LET'S VISIT ITALY

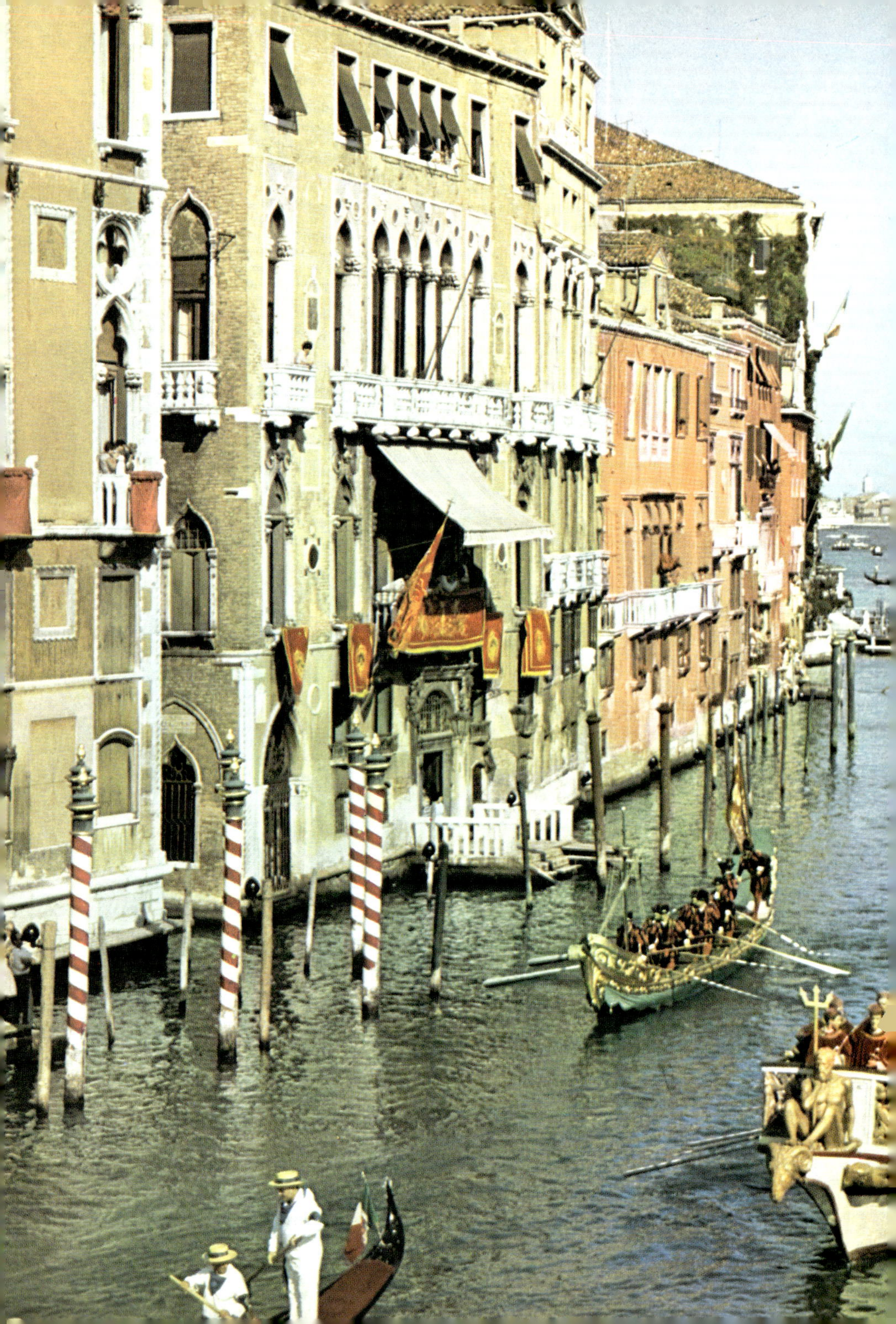

Let's visit ITALY

VERNON BARTLETT

© Vernon Bartlett 1966 and 1972
First published July 1966
Second revised edition August 1972
Reprinted October 1976

All rights reserved. No part of this publication may be reproduced, stored in a retrieval system, or transmitted, in any form or by any means, electronic, mechanical, photocopying, recording or otherwise, without the prior permission of Burke Publishing Company Limited or Burke Publishing (Canada) Limited.

ACKNOWLEDGEMENTS

The Author and Publishers are particularly grateful to Count S. Fago-Golfarelli and the Ente Nazionale Italiano per il Turismo for assistance in obtaining illustrations for this book. They thank the following individuals and organisations for permission to reproduce copyright photographs:

Gaetano Barone; Douglas Dickins; ENIT, Rome; EPT della Spezia e di Massa Carrara; FIAT; FIREMA; Fotolink Picture Library; Keystone Press Agency Ltd.; Michelino, Carrara, and Publifoto, Milan.

ISBN 0 222 66861 X Hardbound
ISBN 0 222 66849 0 Library

Burke Publishing Company Limited,
14 John Street, WC1N 2EJ.
Burke Publishing (Canada) Limited,
91 Station Street, Ajax, Ontario L1S 3H2.
Made and printed by offset in Great Britain by
William Clowes & Sons, Limited, London, Beccles and Colchester

Contents

Map	6
Who Are the Italians?	7
Rome: From a Village to an Empire	13
Popes and Emperors	22
Italy Wins Her Freedom	29
Italy Up to Date	35
A Visit to the North	42
Central Italy	58
Down South	75
Ciao!	89
Index	94

SWITZERLAND
AUSTRIA
FRANCE
VENETIA
PIEDMONT
LOMBARDY
Turin
Milan
Trieste
Venice
R. PO
YUGOSLAVIA
Genoa
Bologna
Ravenna
La Spezia
Italian Riviera
Pisa
Florence
R. ARNO
San Marino
ADRIATIC SEA
UMBRIA
TUSCANY
Perugia
ELBA
R. TIBER
CORSICA
ABRUZZI
Rome
TYRRHENIAN SEA
APULIA
Naples
Salerno
CAPRI
Taranto
SARDINIA
CALABRIA
Palermo
Messina
SICILY
NORTH AFRICA
MALTA
ITALY
0
50
100

Who Are the Italians?

One of your first surprises in Italy will be to find how many other foreigners are there. The country has a population of over fifty-five millions, but every year more than thirty million foreigners cross its frontiers for a few days, weeks or months. Why so many? Because no other country can offer so great a variety of attractions.

Since the beginning of history, foreigners have streamed into Italy. Those who go there today go as friends, but most of the earlier ones went as enemies, out to steal, to destroy, to kill. Look at the map, and you will realise why this should have been so.

From earliest times, the Mediterranean Sea has been one of the busiest stretches of water in the world. Our civilisation comes from the countries along its shores—the very word "civilisation" is derived from Latin, and Latin was one of the languages of the early Italians. The alphabet, arithmetic, the compass, the art of printing, the basis of our laws—almost everything, in fact, which makes it possible for us to live our normal lives—came to us from the Mediterranean or, through the Mediterranean countries, from distant parts of Asia. It is only within the last few centuries, since the Italian, Christopher Columbus, discovered America, that power and wealth have moved from the Mediterranean to the Atlantic.

And there, right in the middle of the Mediterranean, is Italy—a long, narrow strip of land looking rather like a man's leg from the knee downwards. Just off the toe of the Italian mainland is the Italian island of Sicily. Together, they stretch more than half-way across the Mediterranean to Africa. Indeed, millions of years ago, there must have been land all the way across, for the water between Sicily and the African coast is much shallower than that of the western or eastern Mediterranean.

Thus the earliest explorers, sailing from Greece, Egypt or Asia Minor in search of wealth and adventure, could hardly have missed Italy. They came in ships, many of which were rowed by more than a hundred men at a time. Some of these crews settled in colonies in southern Italy, just as, many centuries later, hundreds of Englishmen followed the early Atlantic explorers, and settled in colonies along the east coasts of America. The Greek colonies, indeed, became so important that Sicily and the Italian mainland as far north as Naples became known as *Magna Grecia*—Greater Greece. There are more ancient Greek monuments there today than there are in Greece itself, some of the finest of them being at Paestum, only some forty miles south of Naples.

While the Greeks (and also the Phoenicians, who came

The Temple of Neptune at Paestum

from the countries we now know as Syria and the Lebanon) were settling in southern Italy, other foreigners were crossing the Alps, that great range of mountains which cuts Italy off from Switzerland, France and Austria. These foreigners were moving across Europe from different parts of Asia, driven on by fear of their neighbours, by the spirit of adventure or by the hope of finding land richer than their own. Many of them went as far as the Atlantic coast or crossed the narrow sea to Britain. Others, attracted by the sun, turned southwards. They swarmed up over the mountain passes and down to the rich, warm plains of northern Italy. Finally, pushed on by other migrating tribes, they spread farther and farther down the peninsula until they came into contact with the Greeks, moving up from the south.

All this happened a very long time ago, and we cannot now tell who were the original inhabitants of Italy and who were the newcomers. This mystery is particularly important in the case of the Etruscans, who gave their name to Tuscany, a large region in central Italy. The paintings and objects found in their underground tombs show that they were a highly civilised people, but nobody has yet been able to understand their language. It was against the Etruscans that Horatio defended the bridge across the Tiber.

And the founders of Rome itself? You know the legend that it was founded by Romulus and Remus who, as small children, were nourished by a she-wolf? That is the legend; the historical probability is that the town was founded by a tribe called the Latins, whose language, in a rather different form and with a very different pronunciation, some of you learn in school. They had three special reasons for building Rome just where they did. One was that there is a small island there which made it relatively easy to build bridges across the Tiber; a second was that the largest ships of those days could come that far up the river; a third reason was that, being only sixteen miles from the open sea, the Romans could make shallow tanks to hold sea water which evaporated in the hot sun, leaving them with that very valuable article, salt, which they could sell at a large profit to tribes farther inland. One of the great Roman roads from the city was, and still is, called the Via Salaria, the Salt Road.

Take another look at your map; it helps to explain not only why so many foreigners in early times settled in Italy, but also why so many foreign visitors go there for their holidays.

Up in the north, there are the Alps, the highest mountains in Europe, dividing Italy from the rest of the Continent. But you will also see another range of mountains, the Apennines, which stretch down the country from the extreme north-west to the extreme southern tip. At Gran Sasso, east of Rome, these Apennines reach a height of almost 9,600 feet, or more than twice that of Scotland's Ben Nevis.

Winter at Sestriere, one of Italy's most beautiful mountain resorts

These mountains affect Italy in three ways. One: they provide some splendid winter sports. Two: they provide great varieties of scenery. Three: they make it difficult to get from one part of the country to another; as a result, through many centuries, people have kept their different ways of talking, of cooking, even of thinking, to a much greater extent than they have done in other countries.

One last look at the map. From it, you will see that Italy stretches from north to south for just over seven hundred miles, though the average width is only about ninety miles. Thus, there are many hundred miles of coast-line and also great differences of climate. Milan, in the north, often has fogs almost as thick as those of London, whereas there are places in the south which are nearly as hot and barren as the deserts of North Africa. In summer, you can bathe for most of the day in a sea that is too warm, or you can put on your thickest clothes to keep out the cold in the mountains in the evening. There is nothing dull or monotonous about Italy.

Rome: From a Village to an Empire

There is a well-known saying that "Rome was not built in a day". It certainly was not. The ruins of what is generally called Ancient Rome, which attract hundreds of thousands of visitors every year, cover a period of seven or eight hundred years. Rubbish and rubble are always piling up on waste land, and Rome is so old that, in places, its earliest paving-stones are some forty feet below the present level of the ground.

The few shepherds who built their huts along the banks of the River Tiber 750 years before the birth of Christ soon became powerful. Their mud huts were replaced by stone buildings; the large square stones were fitted on top of each other without the help of mortar to hold them together. Ancient Rome had no shortage of labour; in those days there was no doubt about what would happen to a defeated enemy—the men and women who could be useful were brought back as slaves, and the conquerors took over all their cattle. (The Latin word for money, *pecunia*, was taken from the word *pecus*, a sheep, for these farm animals were largely used instead of hard cash.) So Rome became rich.

Their wealth made their neighbours jealous. Although some of Rome's earliest kings were Etruscans, Etruria became one of Rome's toughest enemies. There were many other tribes who also fought the Romans, but all were defeated by them. Some 350 years after the foundation of the Eternal City, as it is deservedly called, enemies appeared even from the unknown countries north of the Alps. The Gauls, ancestors of the modern French, marched all the way down Italy and even captured part of Rome. They failed to capture the heart of the city, the Capitol. According to legend, they would have done so by surprise attack one night if the geese on the Capitol hill, more alert than the Roman sentries, had not given the alarm.

Such crises did not delay Rome's progress for long. In a little more than a hundred years after the attack by the Gauls—and a hundred years is a short period in the history of a city—the Romans controlled practically all the "leg" of Italy. In another 150 years, they were fighting the Carthaginians for the control of the Mediterranean.

Carthage, the ruins of which are near Tunis, in North Africa, had been built by the Phoenicians, who had emigrated there from the eastern Mediterranean. They governed not only most of North Africa, but also the islands of Corsica, Sardinia and Sicily. They were, therefore, a dangerous threat to Roman ships, especially as they had a superb navy. They had, however, practically no army. The Romans, on the other hand, had a superb army but practically no navy. War between them was difficult, but they fought each other on and off for twenty years or so. In order to be able to attack Rome by land, the great Carthaginian general, Hannibal, conquered Spain and then marched an army (including elephants which he used almost as armies of today use tanks) along the coasts of Spain and France, and over the Alps into Italy.

Despite the difficulty of getting supplies, this amazing man then advanced half-way down Italy, and defeated the Romans at Lake Trasimene (along the shores of which the trains now pass on their way between Rome and Florence).

Most Italian cities and towns today boast a commemorative statue to one of the Roman emperors, like this one in Ravenna

To convince his compatriots of the importance of his victories, he sent back to Carthage three bushels of gold rings taken from the fingers of slaughtered Romans. Then he sat down and waited for more supplies, so that he could capture Rome. But his compatriots showed little interest in a war so far from home, and they gave the Romans time to reorganise. Instead of building up another army to fight Hannibal, they built a fleet with which they attacked Carthage itself.

The Carthaginians at once called on Hannibal to return home. But, by the time he arrived, the Romans were well established on the North African coast; this time they defeated him. He escaped into exile, in the hope that his people would be less harshly treated if he were out of the way. After a siege lasting three years, Carthage surrendered and the Romans spent seventeen days burning and destroying the city. It was never rebuilt, although the Romans themselves later founded a colony near its ruins.

For the next five hundred years, Rome was everywhere victorious. In the days of Julius Caesar, the greatest of her generals, the Roman Empire stretched as far north as Britain, as far west as Portugal, as far east as the Black Sea and as far south as the African coast, all the way from the Atlantic to Egypt. Her trade extended far beyond the frontiers of this empire. For example, silk which had been made in China for at least 2,500 years was imported by the Romans in large quantities. Later, the silkworm was introduced into Italy; to this day, especially in northern Italy, there are rows and rows of mulberry trees, on the leaves of which the silk-worms feed.

* * *

The first rulers of Rome were kings, elected by the patricians—the heads of the most important families. They had much more power than most kings have today, but they were to some extent controlled by the Senate, which consisted of the older patricians. (The word "Senate" comes from *senex*, the Latin word for an old man.) A second class of Romans, the plebeians, had no power at all in the early days. For centuries the State was weakened by the struggle between the patricians, anxious to keep their privileges, and the plebeians, who were anxious to share them. There is much in the history of Ancient Rome which very closely resembles the history of Great Britain during the last thousand years.

After some 250 years of monarchy, Rome became a republic, but the struggle between these two classes continued, with each side trying to get the support of the army, or of the general who controlled it. Julius Caesar, having won victories in different parts of the empire, came to power in this way, after defeating another general, Pompey, who was his own son-in-law.

Caesar was a great man, but also a very ambitious one. Protesting that he did not want the job, he nevertheless managed to get himself appointed the first emperor. But his ambition gave him enemies and he was murdered by jealous senators, one of whom was Brutus, who had been his closest friend. Caesar was only fifty-six years old when he died, but it was claimed that his armies had captured eight hundred cities and defeated three million enemy soldiers. He was the first of a long line of emperors, lasting for over five hundred years but lessening in power as time went by. Britain broke away from the empire in the year 407; elsewhere, enemies nibbled away the outer edges of the empire and the emperors were too weak to turn them back.

This slow collapse of the Roman Empire was due partly to the luxury and laziness of the ruling class. Rome had become too rich. The emperor was said to have about 20,000 slaves, and many aristocrats did not know all their slaves by sight. If you arrive in Rome by train today, you will see an impressive example of this luxury as soon as you leave the station (which, by the way, is one of the most magnificent railway stations in all Europe). There, in front of you, are the ruins of the Baths of Diocletian, emperor at the beginning of the fourth century A.D. There is not very much left, beyond some immense brick walls, to show how the Ancient Romans lived, but at one time the distance round the Baths was about one mile. Besides the different kinds of baths, there were gymnasiums, cafes, places for various games and forms of gambling. Rich Romans spent much of their time in the baths. These were well heated by stoves in the cellars, from which hot air rose through tubes built into the walls. As you know, this is a system adopted by many modern architects.

Trajan's Forum, as it appears today

Most of the slaves in Rome were prisoners of war. There was a great public holiday when some successful general was granted a "triumph". The general would ride through the city with his troops, his prisoners, his captured cattle and carts packed with loot. Most of the prisoners would then be sold in the forum, which was a general market and meeting-place. On this page you can see the Forum of Trajan, built eighteen centuries ago. At that time it must have been crowded with men discussing war and politics, and with women doing their shopping; nowadays, it is deserted except for a fantastic number of cats.

Many of the prisoners were sent to the amphitheatres,

The Colosseum, the most famous amphitheatre of Ancient Rome

where they had to fight for their lives, either against other prisoners or against wild animals, brought over in huge numbers from Africa. The most famous amphitheatre was the Colosseum. Its upper gallery has now collapsed on one side, but when it was in use it held about 50,000 spectators—about half as many as the Wembley Stadium—and awnings could be stretched right across it to protect the spectators from the hot sun. The fighters were called gladiators; some became professionals, much as football or baseball players do nowadays. A defeated fighter could appeal for his life and, if they considered that he had fought bravely, the spectators stretched out their arms with their thumbs held upwards.

The Appian Way, one of the roads from Ancient Rome

His life was then spared. So it is from Ancient Rome that we get the expression, "thumbs up"!

Almost every city in Italy has something to remind its citizens that their country was for so long the leader of the world. Possibly these reminders explain why every Italian likes to put up a show in public. He may live in the smallest, poorest house, but when he appears in the street he will be dressed in his finest clothes—he must not let his ancestors down.

Popes and Emperors

Less than a century after the murder of Julius Caesar in Rome, an almost unknown man was murdered in the Roman colony of Judaea, the country we now call Israel or Palestine. The Roman governor was not very interested—he just knew that there was some trouble between two groups of Jews. The Jewish authorities under his control seemed to be very worried by the revolutionary ideas preached by this man, Jesus, the son of a carpenter in Nazareth; but that was their affair. Doubtless, it would all blow over in a few days. So the governor, Pontius Pilate, washed his hands of it, and Jesus was killed, nailed to a wooden cross on a hill just outside Jerusalem.

But the affair did not blow over. Jesus had preached gentleness, patience, forgiveness and love; and this was in an age of great cruelty, when people found it amusing to watch others being torn to pieces by lions in their amphitheatres. (The Colosseum, by the way, was not built until some years after

St Peter was the first to hold the office of pope. His throne is occupied today by Pope Paul VI, seen here at the opening of the Ecumenical Council

the death of Jesus.) And, since most people wanted to be allowed to live their lives quietly, whereas the government wanted them to fight its wars, or at least to pay for them without protest, the teachings of Jesus won a lot of support, especially among the poor.

23

Rome was then the centre of the world, so it was natural that the leaders of this new religion should come to Rome. There they were treated as enemies of society; many were tortured and killed because they refused to give up their faith. The most important of these martyrs were St Peter (who had been appointed the first bishop of Rome) and St Paul. Others, too, spread the words of Christ; Rome became not only the capital of the Roman Empire, but also of the Christian religion. The early Christians were often persecuted, but the more people are made to suffer for something in which they believe, the stronger their belief becomes. Christianity gained so much ground that, some three hundred years after the death of Christ, even the Roman emperor, Constantine, was converted to Christianity.

We have already mentioned the difficulties experienced by the Romans—as also, very much later, by the British—in keeping control of a huge empire which included people of many races in many parts of the world. At the time when Constantine became a Christian, his empire was breaking up, which is not surprising if you remember that, in those days, the quickest way to send an order to some remote colony was to send it by a despatch rider on horseback. So, while Rome was accepting Christianity, it was losing control of many parts of the world it had previously governed. The empire split into two parts, one of which was still dependent on Rome, while the other part was governed from Constantinople, or Istanbul as that lovely city is now called.

Much worse than that, people from eastern and central Europe—people far less civilised than the Romans—invaded Italy. They finally captured Rome itself, destroying its wealth and its luxury, and appointing one of their own rulers as emperor. For some four hundred years, the Romans lived through a grim, dark age during which much of their civilised way of life was forgotten. At one time—in the year 546—the city's population is said to have been only five hundred.

Meanwhile, a strange thing was happening—Christianity, which earlier emperors had tried so hard to destroy, came to the rescue of the empire. Many of these invaders became Christians and, on Christmas Day, in the year 800, Charlemagne, the greatest of these non-Romans, had himself crowned by the Pope, as the head of the Christian church was now called. Charlemagne was much more at home in northern France and northern Germany than in Rome, but he needed the help of the Pope, and he decided to call his empire, which covered nearly all western Europe, the Holy Roman Empire. That name—Holy Roman Empire—lasted for nearly a thousand years, although the empire often changed shape and size, and had very little to do with Rome. Twenty-eight of its emperors were crowned at Aachen, a German town near the frontiers of Belgium and Holland. From the military point of view, Rome had ceased to be very important; from the religious point of view, its influence was increasing all over Europe.

The emperors, busy in northern Europe, had little time for

Rome itself. More and more, they left the government of Italy to the popes. Indeed, for a thousand years, the popes governed the whole of central Italy, from coast to coast, the country they governed being known as the Papal States. Outside these Papal States, government was more difficult; there was nobody to keep the local strong men in order.

As in England in feudal times, each great family had its own private army, the members of which could take refuge in one or other of the family's castles when some still stronger private army was in the neighbourhood. These ruined castles, dotted all over Italy, provide one of the country's principal attractions to visitors today. The local rulers whose castles controlled important roads and mountain passes became very rich by making travellers pay heavily to cross their land. The emperors were too busy and the popes were too weak to keep them in check. Italy became a country of small, rival states. This is one reason why the country became united only a little over a hundred years ago.

Difficulties between the popes in Rome and the emperors in Aachen or elsewhere became more and more frequent. Often the small Italian states were dragged in on one side or the other. Worse than that, the people inside each little state were divided into supporters of the emperor and supporters of the pope. Thus, for centuries, the leading families in Italy were divided between Guelphs, who supported the popes, and Ghibellines, who supported the emperors. These two names are not even Italian—they were taken from Germany

—but they stand for generations of misery and of bloodshed.

Despite these quarrels, some of these states became very rich and powerful. The Republic of Venice, for example, controlled the eastern Mediterranean. Its principal rival was another Italian republic—that of Genoa, on the other side of the "leg" of Italy. Many years ago, I was travelling along the River Dniester, near the south-west corner of Russia, and I came across the ruins of an immense fortress built there by

The Palazzo della Signoria, the city hall of Florence

the Genoese, some seven hundred years before. How, one wonders, could they build a place like this, so far from home and with only small ships in which to carry their soldiers and supplies.

The third of the great and wealthy city-states was Florence. Although it had not the advantage of Venice and Genoa of being on the sea, the work of its weavers, its goldsmiths and its jewellers was known all over the world. So, too, were its bankers—banking started in Italy; the very word, "bank" comes from the benches at which the bankers of Florence did their work; the main banking street in London is called Lombard Street, after the bankers of Lombardy.

The most famous of the banking families was that of the Medici, a Florentine family which did more than any other family before or since to encourage the arts. Almost every well-known sculptor or painter of the time came to Florence during the years when the Medici ruled that city. It is owing to the encouragement of the Medici that Florence today attracts more artists and art-lovers than any other city of its size.

Italy Wins Her Freedom

In the days of Dante, Italy's greatest poet, early in the fourteenth century, there were no fewer than sixty small states in the area north of the Papal States. Most of these states were controlled by rich and powerful families. But they were so often at war with each other that foreign invaders were easily able to conquer them. Early in the eighteenth century almost all northern Italy came under Austrian rule. In Naples and the south the people had never been free and, from 1522 onwards, they were almost continuously ruled by Spaniards.

So, although Italian was the language spoken all the way through the country, the Italians had very little hope of freedom until, in the first years of the last century, Napoleon conquered most of Europe. He drove the Austrians, the Spaniards and even the pope out of Italy, and governed the whole country through various members of his family.

This was a great step forward in Italian history, but it was not one that pleased the Italians at the time. They wanted national unity, but not unity under foreign rule. In any case, this unity did not last long, since the British and the Prussians defeated Napoleon at Waterloo in 1815, and Italy was again divided. Most of the northern third of the country came again under Austrian rule; the southern third came again under the Spanish Bourbons; the middle third was ruled by the pope. He was an Italian, it is true, but he governed with the help of foreign soldiers.

Hatred of this foreign control produced three great Italian patriots—Mazzini, son of a professor of medicine at Genoa; Garibaldi, son of a fisherman at Nice; and Cavour, member of an aristocratic family in Piedmont, in the north-western corner of the country. These three men are looked upon as the creators of modern Italy.

Mazzini was the man who planned the revolts against the foreign rulers, and he did much of this planning from London, where he lived in exile and in poverty. Garibaldi was the man of action. He recruited a lot of young patriots to form what he called his Legion and, when they were driven out of Italy, many of them joined him in fighting for the independence of Brazil and the Argentine. He was something of a showman, and went around dressed in a red shirt and a loose, white cloak, with a large sword clanking at his side, but he was very tough and brave.

These men had to face years of defeats and disappointments. Then, in 1848, King Louis Philippe of France was overthrown, and this important event led to revolutions all over Europe. Garibaldi and Mazzini were not going to let the opportunity escape them. Garibaldi got together a scratch army to invade Lombardy (the country round Milan) and Venetia (the country round Venice). He had the support of Count Camillo Cavour, prime minister of Piedmont, who hoped that his king, Carlo Alberto of Sardinia and Piedmont, might ultimately become king of a united Italy.

Carlo Alberto's army and Garibaldi's Legion were awkward allies. Everything went wrong with their campaign, and they were badly defeated. Carlo Alberto handed over the crown to his son, Victor Emmanuel II, and went off into exile. Garibaldi managed to escape across the mountains into Switzerland. The independence of Italy seemed to be a long, long way away.

Cavour, indeed, realised that it would be achieved only if the Italian patriots had help from outside. In this, he differed from both Mazzini and Garibaldi. Cavour distrusted Mazzini anyhow because he was a republican and was not particularly interested in the aims of Victor Emmanuel. Garibaldi, on the other hand, thought liberty could be won by his ill-disciplined and unorganised Legion. These three men agreed that Italy must be free, but they disagreed entirely as to how freedom could be won and what sort of government Italy should have when she was free.

Cavour's chance to get help from outside came about in an

unexpected way. To most people in Great Britain, the Crimean War is memorable mainly on account of the Charge of the Light Brigade. To Italians it is memorable because Cavour, by sending some troops to fight on the side of England and France against Russia, was able to win their sympathy for Italy in her struggle for independence.

The French king at this time was Napoleon III, nephew of the great Napoleon who had made himself king of Italy, and had appointed members of his family to rule various parts of it. Why should history not repeat itself? Why should not Napoleon III become king of a united Italy in his turn? He sent a powerful army to help Victor Emmanuel. It defeated the Austrian army, leaving the Austrian emperor in control only of the country round Venice. But history did not repeat itself. The Italian people made it very clear that they wanted Victor Emmanuel as king, and nobody else. So Napoleon withdrew, leaving the Italians to settle with the Austrians as best they could.

Victor Emmanuel now ruled over all northern Italy except the Venice region. But Cavour, his prime minister, was worried by southern Italy and Sicily, where the people were rising in revolt against their own Bourbon king, whose capital was in Naples. Victor Emmanuel was not yet ready to take over the south, but where would the idea of a united Italy be if the south formed a kingdom or a republic of its own?

Cavour and the king were not certain how to act; Garibaldi was. It was enough for him that the people were in revolt in

Sicily. Against Cavour's wishes, he got together a thousand ragged, untrained and almost unarmed Redshirts. On May 5th, 1860, he sailed with them from Quarto (now a very popular bathing beach), just outside Genoa. By the time he reached Marsala, at the western tip of Sicily, the revolt was all but crushed. Nevertheless, his strange army was so warmly welcomed by the people that he captured the island's capital, Palermo, in less than three weeks. In less than five months his ragged army, which included several British volunteers, had advanced up the "leg" of Italy to the Volturno river, north of Naples, and the king, Ferdinand II—generally known as "King Bomba", because his troops had once bombarded the chief Sicilian cities during a period of unrest—had fled.

Now King Victor Emmanuel and Cavour had to act; there was too great a danger that otherwise Garibaldi might make himself king or president of southern Italy. Victor Emmanuel led an army down through the territory of the Papal States, and met Garibaldi outside a little village inn north of Naples. Here Garibaldi made the noblest of many gestures. He greeted Victor Emmanuel as his king, rode at his side into Naples, and called upon the people to cheer, not him, but their new ruler, the ruler of united Italy. Then, refusing titles, honours and money, this creator of a nation went off, with his son Menotti, to the island of Caprera, at the northern tip of Sardinia, where he had a small farm. He took with him nothing but some seed, dried fish, sugar and coffee. Every-

33

thing else he left to the man he had helped to make king of Italy.

Garibaldi later played some part in getting the Austrian rulers out of Venice, and he was then involved in two expeditions to put an end to the Papal States, since the pope still did not recognise Victor Emmanuel as king of all Italy. These expeditions were badly planned and badly timed. They failed, and Garibaldi's influence in his own country was sadly diminished. But he still remained a hero in the eyes of the masses. He visited England, where he was welcomed so enthusiastically that Queen Victoria was very angry—how could she keep on normal and friendly terms with the king of Italy if her people showed such enthusiasm for an Italian who was in disgrace?

After each setback, Garibaldi went back to his small farm. It was there that he died, almost forgotten. But Italian forgetfulness and ingratitude did not last. I doubt whether there is a town in the whole country which does not have a monument, street or square named in his memory.

The monument to Garibaldi on Rome's Janiculum Hill

Italy Up to Date

Italy became a united kingdom in 1860; and yet unity was still not complete. Outside it, but geographically in its centre, there were still the Papal States. True, like most popes, Pius IX was an Italian, but he was not prepared to give up his territory, even to an Italian king.

This territory no longer stretched right across Italy, as it had done for a thousand years or so. By 1861, so many of its former states had broken away to join the Kingdom of Italy that all that remained of the pope's temporal power (that is to say, of the land he governed) was a little strip, not much more than a hundred miles long and thirty miles wide, along the west coast. In the middle of this strip was Rome; and the Italians wanted Rome as their capital. Florence, the temporary capital of Victor Emmanuel's kingdom, was a city with a great past, but not one that could compare with the past of the Eternal City.

People all over the world felt sympathy for the new Italy. Equally well, people all over the world disliked the idea that the Papal States, with so long a history behind them, should disappear. Most of the pope's troops were French, and Victor Emmanuel could not afford to offend the French king, Napoleon III, who had helped to make him king of Italy.

So ten long and frustrating years went by before unity could be completed. Then in 1870, the Franco-Prussian war broke out, and Napoleon III had many other things to think about besides the Italian problem. He needed all the French soldiers he could get to fight against the Prussians, and it was clear he must withdraw those whose job it had been to defend the Papal States. On September 20th, 1870, Italian artillery blew a breach in the walls of Rome—walls that had been built in the days of the Emperor Aurelian, sixteen hundred years earlier—and Italian soldiers took over the city without any serious fighting. At long last, unity was complete.

Pope Pius IX took defeat badly. He shut himself up in the Vatican Palace, at the side of St Peter's, and he stayed there

St Peter's, Rome. The Vatican Palace is on the right of the photograph

By contrast with Mussolini's fascisti, *Italian youth of today is being led along more peaceful and constructive paths. These young men are studying electronics*

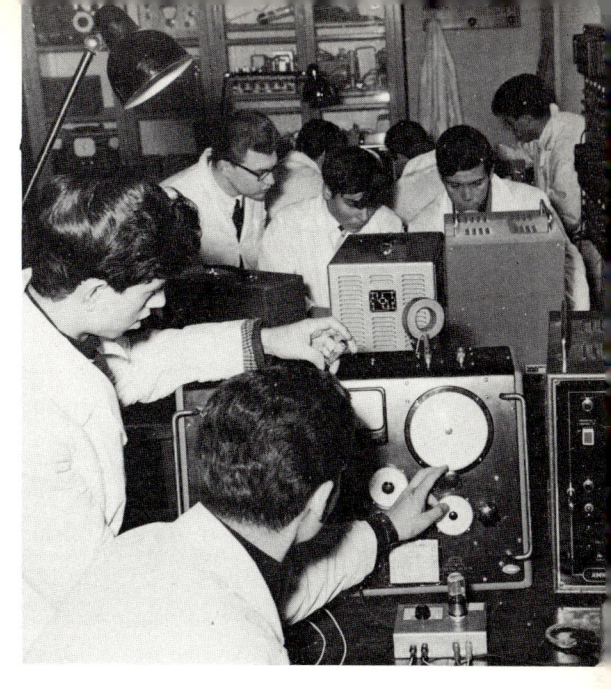

for the rest of his life. It is only within the last few years that popes have moved freely outside the high walls which surround the 108 acres of the Vatican. Pope Pius IX, indeed, ordered Roman Catholics to take no part in Italian politics and, although this ban could not last, the division of Italians into supporters of the pope and supporters of the Italian government has been one more obstacle in the path leading to real national unity.

England has had a parliament for some seven hundred years, and the Act of Union between England and Scotland was signed in 1707. So the British have had time in which to develop a fairly settled form of government. The Italians have not. People were only just beginning to forget the differences between one part of the country and another, and

37

between the pope and the king, when the First World War broke out. At the end of it, Italy was left with vast debts, unemployment, thousands of war cripples and a people on the verge of revolution.

In such circumstances, the parliamentary form of democracy broke down. Government after government was too weak to prevent shocking profiteering on the one hand and absurd strikes on the other. A journalist called Mussolini, who edited a Socialist newspaper in Milan, organised young people into a militant movement which he called Fascism, from the *fasces*, or bundles of rods, which had been the symbol of authority in the days of Ancient Rome. A large number of decent young men and women joined this new movement, but it soon became an army of cheap bullies, as did also the Nazi movement in Germany some twelve years later. Mussolini's Black-shirts and Hitler's Brown-shirts spent much of their time beating up anyone who disagreed with them, but the democratically elected governments in both countries had been so ineffectual that too few people were prepared to resist the bullies.

In October 1922, the Fascists marched on Rome. Mussolini arrived next day by train and Victor Emmanuel III, grandson of Italy's first king, called on him to form a new government. By degrees, all opposition was suppressed. Most of the older political leaders in Italy today spent years of their youth either in exile or in one of Mussolini's detention camps.

What happened to Mussolini happens to every dictator—he was able to act more quickly than any parliamentary government could have done, because there was nobody to oppose him. But in time he lost touch with the people, as no parliamentary government is likely to do. He surrounded himself with flatterers who told him only the things he liked to hear. He grew to distrust the masses and, finally, to hate them. And they grew to distrust and hate him.

His ideas made him unpopular in Britain and the United States, but popular in Nazi Germany. When the Second World War broke out in 1939, he kept out of the war until France was defeated by Germany. He then, in all haste, declared war on France. This gave him, for the time being, a nice feeling of being on the winning side, but it was not what the Italian people wanted. In the First World War, they had fought against Germany; they saw no point in fighting *for* Germany in the Second.

The Americans, the British and their allies landed in Sicily, and many Italians joined them. To check these desertions, Mussolini ordered the execution of several of his closest colleagues, even including his own son-in-law. Had he resisted the temptation to kick France when she was down, his enemies would not have had to land in Sicily and to fight their way all up the "leg" of Italy. Their campaign lasted nearly two years, during which millions of Italians found themselves near the fighting-line on one side or the other, or were bombed by allies or enemies. The damage, especially in central Italy, was immense. One still, today, sees isolated farmhouses with walls pitted with bullet holes. The cities now show few signs of war, but many were very badly damaged.

In Florence, to take one example, five of the six bridges over the River Arno were destroyed. The exception was the Ponte Vecchio, one of the most famous bridges in the world—built in the fourteenth century, and with little shops along each side of it. The Germans spared this bridge but they blew up every building near it to delay the advance of the Allied armies.

So the Italians were forced to fight, first, on the side of Germany. Then they had two governments—a pro-German one in the north and an anti-German one in the south. Towards the end of the war, thousands of young Italians in the north had joined the resistance movement, and were hiding in the mountains, coming down at night to attack German convoys and installations. In April 1945, some of

The Ponte Vecchio in Florence

these partisans, or members of the resistance movement, caught Mussolini when he was trying to escape to Switzerland, and murdered him. The Fascist period was over.

* * *

Recovery from this war has been very difficult. First there was a new obstacle to real national unity. Who were to be the country's new leaders? The older men whom Mussolini had driven into exile? The young partisans? The men who had joined the Fascist party, but had thereby learned something about how to govern a country? What was to be done with those Italians who had been enthusiastic Fascists? Quite apart from the immense material damage done to Italy—the destruction of buildings, bridges, railways and so on—the damage to the ideal of Italian unity was also very great.

One result of the years of Fascism and war was the decision reached in 1946 that Italy should become a republic. This was largely because the king had not shown more courage in checking Mussolini. Italy now has a President, as has the United States of America, and a Senate, which is roughly the equivalent of the British House of Lords, except that all its members are elected and represent the twenty different regions into which the country is divided. There is also a Chamber of Deputies—the equivalent of the British House of Commons. Every Italian of eighteen years and over now has a vote in the election for these deputies.

A Visit to the North

So far, in this book, we have been looking at the Italians, and the influence of their history upon them. Let us now take a closer look at their country. More foreign visitors now arrive by car than by train. Their journey is made very much easier by the fact that there are already two road tunnels under the Alps, which used to cut off almost all road traffic throughout the winter.

The first road tunnel, opened in 1964, passes below the Great St Bernard pass. The famous St Bernard dogs, which used to scramble through the snow to save lost travellers, now have little to do—the travellers are sitting comfortably in their cars thousands of feet below them. The Mont Blanc tunnel, opened in 1965, is the longest road tunnel in the world and it passes under the highest mountain in Europe. The railway tunnels are much longer. The Simplon, for example, is twelve and a quarter miles long; but a railway tunnel, of course, is much narrower than a road tunnel. Thus the Alps have almost ceased to be a barrier between Italy and the rest of Europe.

The Italians, ever since Roman times, have been remarkably good engineers. One of the principal sources of water in Ancient Rome was more than sixty miles from the city, and the water was brought to Rome by aqueduct, raised on arches. This source, the Aqua Marcia, was first used in 145 B.C.; it brings water to Rome to this day.

Nowadays it is, above all, in road-building that the Italian engineers are remarkable. Their motorways, known as *autostrade*, are rapidly breaking down the barriers between north

The *Autostrada del Sole*, crossing the Apennines

On the Milan–Naples *autostrada*

and south. You can now drive from Milan to Reggio Calabria, just opposite Sicily, a distance of almost 800 miles, along a wide motorway, and this is a great achievement in a country where mountains and high hills cover four-fifths of the land. The picture above gives some idea of this road where it crosses over the Apennines between Florence and Bologna.

The government could not possibly pay for all these *autostrade* out of ordinary taxation, so they are built by semi-independent organisations, and the motorists pay for them as they go. Travellers in England, many years ago, used to pay at toll-houses for the right to use the roads; travellers on the *autostrade* pay tolls at very modern check-points, built here and there across the road. There is a picture of one on this page. This is similar to the system employed on the United States turnpikes.

Since these roads are built for speed, they avoid all towns. Most visitors to Italy go there partly to see the splendid architecture in the older towns. So they turn off the *autostrada* on to the older and slower roads. Many of these slower roads are the old Roman roads brought up to date. For example, if I want to drive north or south from my nearest large town,

An *autostrada* toll-gate at Naples

Pisa, I use the Via Aurelia, along which the Roman soldiers must have marched nearly two thousand years ago to garrisons in southern France or Spain.

So much for the roads. Let us now see something of the country through which they pass. Geographically, one can best think of the country in three sections—a very rich plain in the north; a large, agricultural area of beautiful hilly country in the centre; a southern area, dry, mountainous, very beautiful, but still very poor.

All roads into Italy from the north are, of course, very beautiful, since they pass over or through the Alps on their way down to the rich northern plain. Even before the invasion by Hannibal and his elephants, enemy armies came into Italy over the mountain passes. It is not therefore surprising to see the ruins of great castles which used to defend the roads into Italy. Some of these roads lead to Turin.

The castle of Fenis which was used to defend the road into Italy

A view of the Fiat works in Turin

Turin is the home of the great Fiat motor works, which supply nine-tenths of Italy's cars and employ some 50,000 workers. Besides being a very beautiful country, Italy is now one of the great industrial nations of the world.

Turin is also the capital of Piedmont. It is here that Cavour and his king, Victor Emmanuel II, planned the freedom and unity of Italy. It is a city with many elegant palaces and buildings, on the banks of Italy's largest river, the River Po.

With more than a million people, Turin is the fourth city of Italy. Rome now has nearly two millions; Milan has over a million and a half inhabitants; Naples has well over one

47

The fortress of Bard, not far from the modern road which leads from the Mont Blanc tunnel to Turin

million. Thus, two of Italy's four largest cities, Milan and Turin, are in this northern section. They have excellent communications with the rest of Europe, and they are within easy reach of two of Italy's largest ports, Genoa and Venice. This northern plain has some of the richest agricultural land in Europe, but more and more farms are being replaced by factories, and men who used to work on the land in other parts of Italy are crowding into these factories.

The people of Milan, therefore, find it very difficult to think of Rome as the capital of Italy, and certainly they can claim that they add more to Italy's wealth than does any other city. Visitors to Milan, however, are less interested in its factories than in its famous and extraordinary cathedral, and its opera house, La Scala, in which every famous singer during nearly two hundred years has sung. There are also important picture galleries, fine old churches and the Ambrosiana Library to be visited. Milan is a large and very busy city; one cannot blame the visitor if he hurries away as soon as he can northwards to the Italian lakes, westwards to Genoa and the Riviera, eastwards to Venice and Trieste, or southwards to the smaller, quieter cities of central and southern Italy.

Several of the roads and railway lines into Italy pass by these lakes north of Milan, and it is not astonishing that thousands of foreigners, arriving with the intention of seeing the whole country, never get farther south than Stresa, Bellagio or the little towns on the shores of Lake Garda. The gardens near the lakes are filled with the flowers, shrubs and trees you would expect to see in semi-tropical countries, and yet, behind and above them, are the snow-topped mountains of the Alps.

Turin and Milan are both at the foot of the Alps. The great plain of the River Po begins just to the east of the one and to

Milan's extraordinary cathedral

A view of Lake Como

the south of the other; and it stretches across the country to Venice. It has mile upon mile of vines, growing up into the branches of mulberry trees, and the silkworms that live on these trees make Italy the greatest producer of silk in Europe. This part of Italy also produces three cheeses which you have probably seen in your grocer's shop—Gorgonzola, Bel Paese and Parmesan. Where the soil is too wet to grow good wheat, the farmers flood it and grow rice. Every acre is productive.

Small wonder that the road to Venice passes through or near several very rich and famous towns.

There is Padua, with a university dating from the thirteenth century, in which the astronomer Galileo was a professor. Here, too, Dante and Petrarch, Italy's two great poets, were undergraduates. There is Cremona, where the world's most famous violins were made by Stradivarius and others in the seventeenth and eighteenth centuries. There is Verona, scene of two of Shakespeare's plays—you have read about the bitter rivalry between Guelphs and Ghibellines; Romeo's family was Guelph and Juliet's was Ghibelline, and it was this fact which made it so difficult for the two lovers to meet.

A typical Italian scene— row upon row of vines

A Venetian gondola. The Doge's Palace is seen in the background

Venice is, of course, unique. Near the Adriatic, the River Po divides into several channels and into lagoons—lakes of salty water cut off, or nearly cut off, from the sea by sandbanks. Venice lies in one of these lagoons, and its famous Lido is on the long sandbank that protects it from the sea.

It is amazing that Venice exists at all. The city is built on 117 small islands, divided from each other by some 150 canals. The islands are so low that the bridges between them have to be raised well above street level, so that the boats, which carry almost all the traffic, can pass under them. So the only ways of moving about Venice are by boat or on one's own feet. Every house has to be built on scores of piles—great, pointed trunks of trees that have to be driven down

St Mark's Square and
Cathedral, Venice

through yards of mud and into the soil beneath. Thus the cost of building is fantastically high, and the work must have been very difficult in the old days, when there were no steam or motor engines. And yet, as you know, Venice was at one time immensely rich and immensely powerful.

Some of the boats in Venice are also unique. They are long, shallow, black boats with high metal prows and sterns, and are called gondolas. There is a picture of one on page 52, with the Doge's Palace and the tower, or *campanile*, of St

The sea-front at Riccione, on the Adriatic

Mark's in the background. (The *doge* was the president of the Venetian Republic, the word coming from the Latin *dux*, or leader.) Venice can be very cold and damp in winter; it can be very smelly in summer; at any time of year, but especially in spring, it can be incredibly beautiful.

*   *   *

Venice is well to the north of the delta made by the River Po flowing into the Adriatic Sea. South of this delta, the sandy beach runs, with very few breaks, almost the whole way down the coast of Italy. In summer the beaches are covered by mile upon mile of bathing-huts, umbrellas and restaurants. Those who prefer a rocky coast travel westwards, not eastwards, from Milan, to the Italian Riviera. Before we do so, something more must be said about this great plain we have crossed on the journey from Turin to the Adriatic.

Italy, formerly very much handicapped by an almost complete lack of coal, has of recent years very successfully developed its water power. Except for the Po, which winds across this plain, almost all the rivers are short and swift. Thus they are of no use for shipping, but they are very useful for providing electricity. Now there is a new source of power—after the Second World War, engineers sinking wells in search of petroleum came across immense supplies of natural gas under the northern plain, near the lovely old city of Piacenza.

The harbour of Portofino, near Genoa

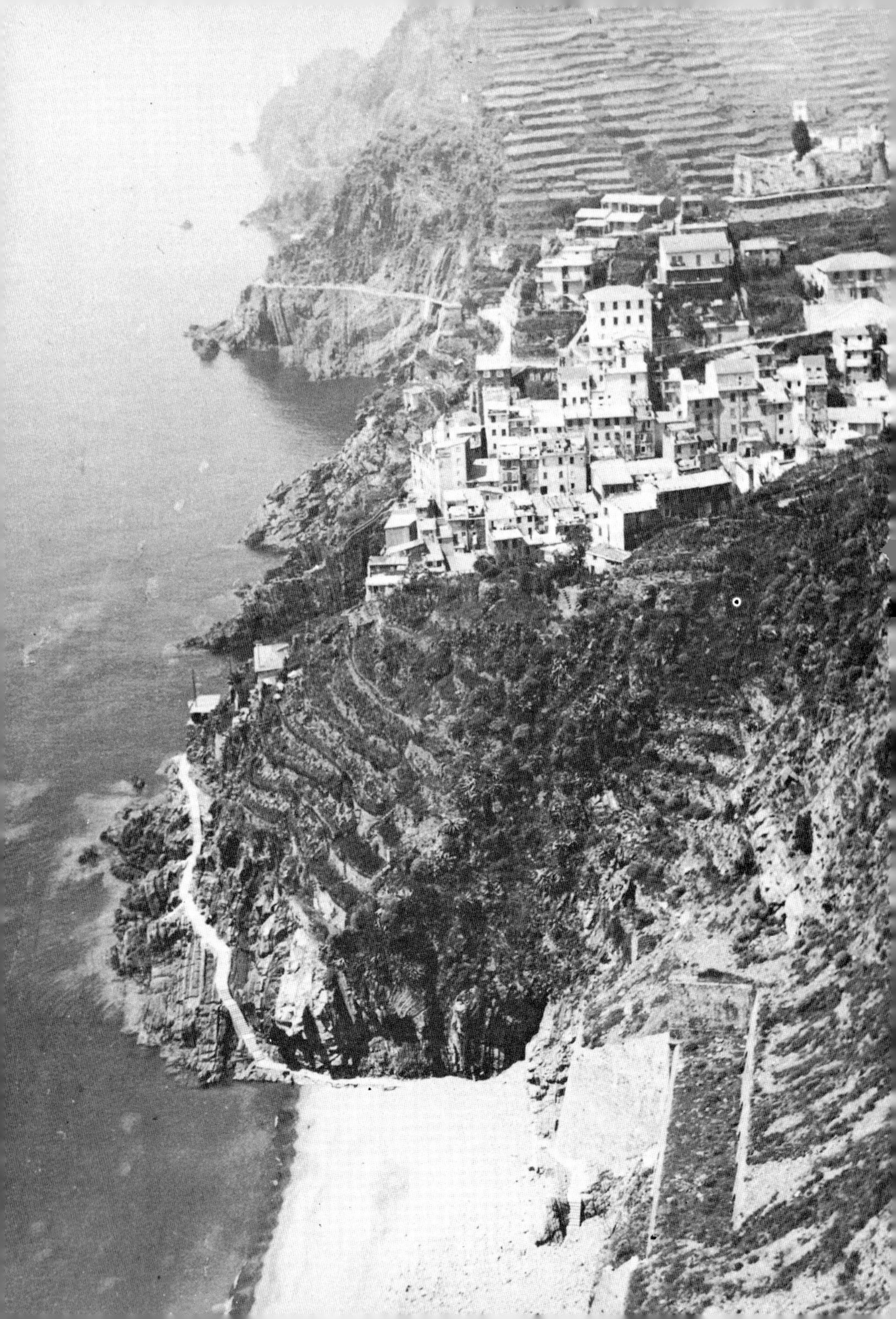

This gas, piped to factories, has added greatly to the wealth of northern Italy, attracting thousands of workers from the centre and the south.

Take another look at your map. You will see that Venice is at the top of the "leg" on one side, and Genoa is at the top on the other. Genoa is the second port in the Mediterranean (Marseilles, in France, being the first). Unlike many ports, Genoa is a very beautiful city, with the mountains rising so steeply behind it that some of its streets have to pass through long tunnels, and the coast on either side of it—to Bordighera and the French frontier on the west, to Rapallo and Portofino on the east—is very lovely.

There is one section of this eastern Riviera which is not yet crowded, mainly because it is so difficult to get to it. This is the stretch of coast known as the *Cinque Terre*, or Five Towns— five villages crouching just above high-water line and at the foot of hills that rise steeply to a height of some two thousand feet. They are all on the main railway from Genoa to Rome, but few trains stop there. The picture on page 56 shows you Riomaggiore. You can see the terraces on which vines are grown, and which rise so steeply that the workers can get from some terraces to others only with the help of ropes or ladders. Nobody who visits the Cinque Terre is ever likely to think of the Italians as lazy people.

Riomaggiore, one of the Five Towns

Central Italy

Let us now drive down the great *autostrada* running southwards from Milan. For the first 120 miles the country is flat and very rich—still a part of the great northern plain. But, far away to the west, we can see the mountains, the Apennines, and at Bologna the road turns suddenly towards them and over them. From Bologna to Reggio Calabria, the road runs through or near mountainous country almost all the way.

Bologna is famous in several respects. It was an important city even in the days of the Etruscans, who captured it some five hundred years before the birth of Christ. It has the oldest university in Europe, said to have been founded in A.D. 425, and it was so well known in the thirteenth century that it had about 13,000 students. Bologna also claims, with some reason, to have the best cooking in Italy.

The Garisenda Tower, one of Bologna's leaning towers

Like Pisa, Bologna has its leaning towers. You know the expression, "keeping up with the Joneses"? These Bologna towers were just that. In the Middle Ages, families tried to show how important they were by building high towers above their houses—the higher the tower, the greater their importance. They can be found in several Italian cities, but nowhere more attractively than in the little hill town of San Gemignano, between Florence and Sienna. Many of them were badly built, and collapsed on to passers-by. In many cities there were by-laws forbidding anybody to build a tower higher than that of the town hall but, even so, they so frequently caused accidents that most of them had to be pulled down. It is probable that the towers of Bologna lean because their builders did not pay enough attention to their foundations, but some experts believe that the architects built them that way to show how clever they were.

If you were not to turn to the right at Bologna, and across the mountains, your road would take you straight on to the Adriatic coast at Rimini. So straight a road that, quite rightly, you might guess that it had been built by the Romans. Most probably, it was along this road that Roman legions marched on their way to invade Britain. But we are bound for Rome, and the best road nowadays is the *autostrada* which winds over the Apennines to Florence. With its scores of viaducts and tunnels, it must be one of the most exciting and most beautiful roads in the world.

We are now in Tuscany, a country of great, rounded hills, covered with pines or chestnut trees. Below these forests comes the silver-grey of the olive groves and, below them again, the row upon row of vines. Dark, slender cypress trees stand around the old farms, many of which are built like fortresses—reminders of the days when this part of Italy was divided into small, rival states, often at war with each other. The fields are small, for the hills are steep, and have to be terraced. Until a few years ago the plough was generally pulled by large, white oxen. The hills remind one of the back-

Viareggio with the "snow-tipped" Apuan Alps in the background

ground of some picture, painted four or five hundred years ago and now hanging in one or other of the world's picture galleries.

In summer, the high hills are dotted with sheep, which are led down to the plains before the winter snows begin. At the change of the seasons, one may meet flock after flock of them on the roads, with a shepherd in front and another in the rear, each carrying a large green umbrella with a red-painted handle. They are the best-behaved sheep I have ever seen, keeping well in to the side of the road, but they are very small by American or British standards, and are bred rather for their wool than for their value as mutton.

A marble quarry above Carrara—the "snow" is actually white marble

North-west from Florence, just south of the Cinque Terre, is an area of mountains quite different from most of the Apennines. The Apennines generally have rounded summits; these mountains between Florence and the sea are all crags and rocks, like the Swiss and Austrian Alps; indeed, they are called the Apuan Alps.

The main road and the main railway between Genoa and Rome pass along the narrow plain between these mountains and the sea, and every traveller along this plain is amazed to see that, even in midsummer, the peaks appear to be covered with snow. The picture on page 61 shows Viareggio, a very popular seaside resort on this plain, with the Apuan Alps in the background. In some lights, the "snow" is much more obvious than it is in this picture. You will see it better on page 62, which helps to explain the mystery of midsummer snow. At the foot of the mountains is a town called Carrara. You have probably heard of Carrara marble; this "snow" is nothing but millions upon millions of chips of white marble.

For more than two thousand years, men have been quarrying this marble, bringing great blocks of it down to the valley on wooden sleds or sending them hurtling down the mountainside in the hope they would not be too damaged when they reached the valley. In Carrara and other towns on the plain, the marble is cut into strips or slabs and exported to different parts of the world. In most cases, the higher one climbs, the whiter the marble, and you can imagine Michelangelo, the most famous of Italian sculptors, clambering

63

Michelangelo's *Pietà* in St Peter's, Rome

around in the mountains in search of perfect pieces. He spent months before he chose the marble for the *Pietà* which is now in St Peter's in Rome.

Before leaving the west coast, one must visit Pisa. The building of the Leaning Tower began in 1174, and more than a hundred years went by before it was finished. It is 179 feet high, and it leans nearly fifteen feet out of the perpendicular. There are endless discussions between the experts as to methods of making sure that its great weight—about 14,000 tons—does not one day bring it crashing to the ground. The tower and its cathedral are built in the style generally known as Central Romanesque, which is the style of many Tuscan churches, and it would attract thousands of visitors even if the tower were not leaning. Many people who climb its two hundred steps find that its angle makes them feel seasick, and are glad to come down again without even stopping to admire the view from the top.

Pisa cathedral and the leaning tower

The two most famous cities of central Italy are, of course, Rome and Florence, the one on the River Tiber and the other on the River Arno.

Florence was the home of what is called the *Rinascimento*, or Renaissance, the rebirth of art in Europe. The artists of the *Rinascimento*, far more than artists at any other period, were men of very wide interests. Michelangelo was a sculptor, a painter, a poet and also an architect. Giotto planned the tower of Florence Cathedral, but he was also a painter of great importance. Brunelleschi, who built the immense dome of this same cathedral, was also a goldsmith. Leonardo da Vinci not only painted many famous pictures, including the Mona Lisa in Paris, but was also an inventor, a geologist and an engineer. One of his inventions was a flying machine; it did not manage to fly, but there cannot have been many other men in history with enough imagination to foresee a development that was not to take place until nearly four hundred years after his death. With such men about, life in the Tuscan cities such as Florence, Sienna and Pisa, or Umbrian cities such as Perugia, Assisi and Spoleto, must have been very stimulating.

Central Italy is famous for its hill towns. At the top of the hill is the castle in which the local ruler lived. Below the castle will be the cathedral, where the people went to pray, and the city hall, where they began to learn how to govern themselves. Crowded inside the high protecting walls of the town will be tall houses, facing each other across narrow

The castle of Fivizzano in the Apuan Alps, typical of the hill towns in central Italy

streets. Each hill town resembles the others, and yet each is so different that it is always worth the extra effort to climb the steep roads that lead to them.

One of these hill towns must, however, have a paragraph to itself. Some sixty miles east of Florence, and fifteen miles from Rimini, on the Adriatic coast, is San Marino, one of the oldest and certainly the smallest republic in the world. It covers thirty-eight square miles. By way of comparison, Staten Island, in New York Harbour, covers rather more than fifty-seven square miles, and the Isle of Wight covers 147. This tiny republic is supposed to have been founded in the fourth century, and it has kept its independence partly because the town is built on three very steep mountain crags which were easy to defend and partly because it developed a very sensible form of government; it is ruled by two "captains regent" (elected for six months) and a small parliament. If you collect stamps, you probably know about San Marino already, for it makes much of its money by issuing its own postage stamps, which visitors in their thousands stick on picture postcards, showing men in San Marino's picturesque uniforms.

* * *

The vines and olives of Tuscany are typical of this hill country. Even the smallest cottage is likely to have a few rows of vines. Actually, most of Italy's wine comes from the south, but Chianti, produced in Tuscany, south of Florence, is probably the best-known Italian wine. In most years, Italy

The grape harvest

makes more wine than any other country—sometimes she comes second to France in quantity, and she is a long way behind France in quality. Men, women and children all drink wine, but one very rarely sees any case of drunkenness in Italy.

More olive oil comes from the south than from Tuscany, but Tuscan oil is said to be the best. The olive trees may live for hundreds of years, and they are cut back each year in a way no other tree could stand. Often their trunks are so split, twisted and gnarled that one wonders how they can remain standing.

Somehow each year, from November to February, they go on producing their fruit, which look like very small, black plums. When these are crushed in the village mill, they give an oil that is almost colourless and tasteless; it is used by Italians and many other people for all their cooking. Much that is not used for cooking is used to make soap or cosmetics.

A third important crop for most small farms is maize, or Indian corn. (The Italians call it *grano Turco*, or Turkish corn.) Some of this maize goes to feed the cattle or the rather scraggy chickens running about the farm, but much of it is ground into a kind of flour called *polenta*, which many Italians eat because it is cheaper than the *macaroni* or *spaghetti* for which they are so famous.

These are the foods on which millions of Italians live—*polenta, pasta* (as all forms of macaroni are called), chestnut flour, or bread dipped in oil and eaten with garlic, onions or tomatoes. Many of them cannot afford much in the way of meat. On this rather unexciting diet, they work very hard indeed. It is true that, especially in the south, everyone has a rest, a *siesta*, during the hottest hours of the day. This makes some foreigners think that the Italians are lazy; these same foreigners are probably still asleep in the morning, when the Italians are already at work.

*   *   *

Almost due south of Florence is Sienna, its great enemy in earlier days. It is a city which no visitor to central Italy ought to miss (but so is Perugia, or Assisi) for no other city in all Italy has a more beautiful open space than the Piazza del Campo, in front of the town hall. Twice a year there are horse-races round this *piazza*, when the representatives of the city's seventeen districts, dressed in mediaeval costumes, com-

The Sienna *palio*, held in the main square

pete for a *palio*, or banner. Another reason for visiting Sienna is that there you will hear the purest Italian—or so the Siennese say.

The chances are that your paintbox has colours called burnt sienna and burnt umber—useful reminders of the great importance to art of Sienna and Umbria, the region east of Sienna. Florence, Sienna and Venice must have produced more great artists than any other three towns in the world, not excepting Paris.

South and west of Sienna, the landscape changes. It becomes severe and rather sad, and few foreigners trouble to visit it. It must at one time have been busy and prosperous, for farmers on the bare hills sometimes come across the burial grounds of their remote Etruscan ancestors. Their tombs are underground, and are reached by steep paths; some of them are decorated with admirable wall paintings which show how civilised these mysterious people must have been. Apparently the Romans got the idea of chariots from the Etruscans, who were great horsemen; their paintings show also that they kept dogs and cats as pets.

Much of the country east of Rome, known as the Abruzzi, is magnificently wild. Here, the Apennines reach a height of almost 10,000 feet, and every winter the newspapers report that the snow has driven the wolves down from the mountains to attack farm animals in the valleys. Here there are far more sheep than in Tuscany, and the wild-looking shepherds play bagpipes, like the Scots. Here, too, is a National Park, where you can—or rather, may if you are lucky—see wild boars or bears. Although the Abruzzi are so far south, the snow lasts from early November to May or June, and yet, farther north, on the Adriatic coast, you will find olives, figs and oranges—fruits one expects to see in a very hot climate.

* * *

And so we come back to the Eternal City. One can divide it into four parts. There is a large and busy new section, for Rome is growing very fast. Its most famous street is the Via Veneto where there are more film stars to be seen than on any other street outside Hollywood. At the other end of the time scale, there is Ancient Rome. Thirdly, there is the Rome of the Vatican, grouped around St Peter's and the Vatican City. And, lastly, there is the Rome of the *Rinascimento*, with

The Spanish Steps which lead to the *Rinascimento* section of Rome—the part of the city which has its origins in the Renaissance

its narrow streets running between high buildings with immense doorways, and large windows on the first floor, known as the "*piano nobile*", or noble floor.

Everyone has his own tastes. For me, Rome begins only when I have come down the Spanish Steps into the city of the *Rinascimento*. There is a picture of this famous staircase on page 72 but it cannot show you the warm and friendly colour of the buildings on either side of it. The young poet, Keats, died in the house on the right of the Steps.

In this old city, between the Spanish Steps and the Vatican there are many large buildings which are dilapidated and decaying. But, if you run the risk of being run over, and stop to stare up at them, you realise how beautiful they are. They may now be slums, with the washing hanging out to dry, but you will be amazed by the dignity of their windows, their carved or painted ceilings, their great, wide staircases. Piazza Navona is generally considered the centre of the old city—in ancient times the Romans ran chariot races round it. In

Piazza Navona in Rome. It was a racecourse in the time of the Ancient Romans

the streets surrounding it there is hardly a building which is less than four or five hundred years old. If you were to dig down here, or in any part of Rome near the Tiber, you would find layer after layer of traces of still older buildings. The Eternal City deserves its name.

The Fontana di Trevi is a favourite place for foreign visitors although it is only a little more than two hundred years old. They come here because, according to tradition, if you throw a coin into the fountain before you have to leave Rome, you will return there one day. As you can imagine, the Romans, and particularly the small boys who live near the Fontana, do nothing to discourage the tradition.

The Trevi Fountain (Fontana di Trevi), Rome

Positano, a seaside town which attracts many visitors from all parts of the world

Down South

Immediately south of Rome are the Alban Hills, dotted with the country villas of the richer Romans and with charming little towns. They are volcanic in origin, but they have been popular holiday places for at least two thousand years. In early days, they were reached by the Appian Way, one of the most famous of Roman roads—St Paul came along this road on his way from Egypt to Rome.

Nowadays the journey southwards is much easier; there is a fine *autostrada* through the mountains to Naples. Inland, to the left of the *autostrada*, the country is very wild indeed, and most of the roads that zigzag across it are marked on the map with a narrow, green line—the sign used by mapmakers to show that the scenery is very picturesque. Already the visitor

75

realises that there is nothing comfortable and easy-going about southern Italy. The people, of course, speak Italian, but otherwise they have little in common with the Italians of the centre and the north. Indeed, when you reach the "heel" of Italy it is easier to believe you are in North Africa than in the same country as Florence or Milan. There are strange houses called *trulli*, with round pointed roofs rather like wigwams. They are very African in appearance, and the songs sung by the workers in the olive orchards and the vineyards are very similar to those heard in Arab countries.

For the moment, our destination is Naples and the wonderful country immediately to the south of it—perhaps the most attractive anywhere in Italy. Pictures of Positano and Amalfi will help to explain why so many visitors come to this region every year. Near these little seaside towns is the famous island of Capri (pronounced with the accent on the first syllable). There are other pleasant little bays farther down

Amalfi, south of Naples

the west coast, but they are rather remote, and it will be some years before their hotels are filled with foreign visitors, or even before there are hotels for the foreign visitors to fill.

Naples has a population of more than a million. The Neapolitans are lively, sentimental, poor and, to all appearances, very cheerful despite their poverty. They sing even more than the people in other Italian cities. Caruso, whose voice you have probably heard on records, was only one of many great singers who once earned a living of sorts by

A typical Neapolitan street scene

A street in Pompeii. The stones in the foreground formed the Ancient Roman version of a pedestrian crossing

singing in the streets and cafés of Naples. You could not feel lonely in Naples; somebody would be sure to speak to you, even if it were only to ask the time, to try to sell you something, to offer to play some Neapolitan music for you on his guitar or, quite frankly, to beg. It is an extremely noisy, lively, crowded and colourful city, built on the slopes of a hill overlooking one of the most beautiful bays in the world. The city is terribly overcrowded, but there is an Italian saying that *dove entra il sole non entra il medico*—"where the sun comes in, the doctor need not come"—and fortunately there is plenty of sun in Naples.

Out across the bay and away to the left is Mount Vesuvius,

with its lazy puff of smoke to remind us that it is still an active volcano; a chair-lift takes visitors to the edge of the crater. At the foot of Vesuvius are Pompeii and Herculaneum, two towns that were buried in ash and lava when Vesuvius erupted in A.D. 79. Herculaneum is, perhaps, the more interesting of the two, but most visitors go to Pompeii, which was a city of twenty thousand inhabitants before it was completely covered with ash, pumice stone and lava. Part of it was buried to a depth of sixty feet; as the ash and lava are dug away, the town is revealed almost exactly as it was on the day of that disaster. Here, and in Herculaneum, you can understand the conditions in which people lived some nineteen centuries ago.

In pictures of Pompeii, you will notice raised stones in the road. They were stepping-stones that allowed pedestrians to cross the road without getting their sandals dusty or muddy; the gaps between the stones were wide enough for the chariot wheels. These pedestrian crossings were to be found at several street corners, much as pedestrian "islands" are found in the middle of the much wider streets of today.

* * *

In many Italian streets you will notice old men, rather fatter and more prosperous in appearance than the average, and decidedly better dressed. If you ask one of them the way, he may reply in broken English, and you will discover that he has lived many years in America and has now come back to his own village to spend the rest of his life in comfort with the help of his American old age pension. It is in the south that the desire, or the need, to emigrate is strongest; in the early years of this century, as many as 600,000 Italians left Italy every year, and most of them came from the south.

If you buy a packet of dried figs, it will probably have a label on it to show that it comes from this part of Italy. I have already mentioned that these southern regions produce more wine and olive oil than any other. Brindisi and Bari, on the Adriatic coast, are busy ports; Taranto, in the "heel", has a great naval base. But southern Italy as a whole is very poor, very short of water, and it can offer few opportunities to its people to earn a decent living.

As long ago as 1931—long before the north had built its fine new factories—over one million Italians who had been born in the south were living in the north, but only 100,000 Italians who had been born in the north were living in the south. The government is now making great efforts to improve roads, water supplies, schools and other public services in the

Tunny fishing in southern Italy

south. It is encouraging business men to build factories there, instead of encouraging southern workers to leave their homes in order to work in factories in Milan, Turin and other northern cities. But many years will go by before southern Italians have opportunities as good as those of their northern compatriots.

It is difficult to remember that this region and the nearby island of Sicily were, at one time, the most prosperous parts of the world. The word "sybarite" means someone who lives in great luxury and comfort. In view of the present southern poverty, it is surprising that the word comes from the name of Sybaris, a very prosperous town not far from Taranto at the time when all this land was part of *Magna Grecia*, well over two thousand years ago.

Since the days of the Greeks, the south has known one period of power and importance, and that was when Frederick II, whose family came from Swabia, in southern Germany, was Holy Roman Emperor. Like so many of the other emperors, he was crowned at Aachen, in north-west Germany, but he spent most of his life in Sicily and southern Italy, where he gave great encouragement to artists, architects, poets and men of learning generally. There is not very much to attract the foreign visitor to the toe or heel of Italy today; for much of what there is, Frederick is to be thanked. His grandiose castles, built more than seven hundred years ago still stand as magnificent monuments above many of the poor and sleepy towns of the south.

A Sicilian market scene

We are back almost at the point from which we started. You may remember reading of the arrival in Sicily of the Greeks and other peoples who set out from the shores of the eastern Mediterranean. We have now to explore that island, which plays so great a part in the legends of the Greeks. Their sailors dreaded the narrow waters between the rocks of Scylla, on the mainland, and the whirlpools that bore the name of Charybdis—for there are, in fact, very strong and dangerous currents in this channel, only two miles wide.

Sicily is less poor than the three regions of southern Italy—

Apulia, Calabria and the Basilicata—and its scenery is so splendid that one is likely to overlook the way in which whole families, and such farm animals as they own, are all crowded into one or two rooms without windows. Here, more than anywhere else in Italy, people pay little attention to the laws made in far away Rome. Instead, they tend to obey the *Mafia*, an extremely powerful secret society which may protect and help those who pay it part of what little money they earn, but which makes life difficult, and even dangerous, for those who do not.

Long ago Sicily attracted foreign invaders of every sort from the eastern Mediterranean and from Carthage; foreigners also came from the Atlantic. At about the time when some

A view of Taormina

An Ancient Greek theatre near Taormina in Sicily

Normans were planning to invade England with William the Conqueror, other members of this tough and adventurous race had settled in Sicily and southern Italy, and to people who are interested in architecture, one of the charms of Sicily is the way in which you may find the work of Norman, Arab and other craftsmen all in one building.

Thus the Sicilians, even more than any other Italians, are a mixture of many races. In addition, they and other southern Italians were ruled by the Spaniards for some six hundred years. They are therefore very different from the other Italians. A Sicilian is a Sicilian first and an Italian second. His island is the largest island in the Mediterranean—being slightly larger than Sardinia—and he is very much aware of the fact.

Some parts of Sicily are very fertile. All of it is very beautiful. On page 84 there is a picture of the ruins of the Greek theatre at Taormina and on this page there is one of a Greek temple at Segesta. If you remember that these great buildings were erected some 2,400 years ago, you will realise how much our present civilisation owes to Greece and Italy.

*   *   *

Sardinia is much more remote than Sicily, and it is only within the last few years that visitors have begun to discover it. Its problems resemble those of the larger island—mountainous country, poor soil, very little water and large estates owned by men who seldom come to look at them. Both islands

An Ancient Greek temple at Segesta, Sicily

have their local parliaments, but these are sometimes used rather to keep things as they are than to carry out drastic and badly needed improvements. Thus, plans made in Rome to build a dam across a valley in Sicily, so that the peasants may at last get a reasonable water supply, may be hindered

A *nuraghe* in Sardinia

by the *Mafia*, some of whose members do well for themselves by selling water to the peasants at a high price. Far too many children either go to no school at all or are taught for only a year or two in unsuitable buildings by teachers who are overworked and underpaid. Far too many landowners, who know that they would have to pay higher wages if their workers were better educated, do nothing to encourage education.

The origin of the Sardinians is nearly as mysterious as that of the Etruscans. They are short, dark and rather proud of their differences from the Italians of the mainland, about which they talk as though it were a foreign country. To Italians from the mainland, the language of Sardinia is strange, being at times closer to Spanish or to mediaeval Latin than to modern Italian. Much of the work on the island is done by dwarf donkeys.

Very little is known of the original inhabitants of Sardinia; they have left nothing behind them to suggest that they had reached a level of civilisation to be compared with that of the Etruscans. But there are some thousands of large round towers known as *nuraghi* in which, apparently, these early inhabitants lived and in which they could defend themselves from invaders.

The third important Italian island, less than one-tenth the size of Sardinia, is Elba, half-way up the west coast and only six miles from the mainland. It is to this island that Napoleon was sent after the defeats that followed his disastrous retreat from Moscow in 1812. He was king of Elba for nine months, after which he escaped and returned to Paris, only to be defeated a few months later at Waterloo. Elba has some of the most beautiful bathing beaches to be found anywhere in the Mediterranean, but it is important to Italians mainly because, at the eastern end of the island, some of the hills consist entirely of iron ore, from which they make their steel. This ore was mined by the Etruscans some 2,500 years ago; if you scramble about in the hills, you may come across lumps of ore which were half-melted in their primitive furnaces. There are said to be 150 different minerals to be found on Elba, and almost every stone you pick up weighs much more than you would have expected, because it is so full of some kind of metal.

Ciao!

Our visit to Italy is almost ended. We have had to do what so many other visitors to Italy have to do—to see too much in too short a time. It is only if you can stay long enough in one place to be accepted as a friend, and not as a tourist, that you can understand the Italians.

They are polite to the tourists, who bring a lot of money into their country. But they cannot always enjoy the way in which millions of foreigners every year crowd their beaches, their roads and their towns, and take photographs of their slums because these slums are "quaint" or "picturesque".

"After all," these Italians may say to themselves, "your ancestors were the slaves of our ancestors some two thousand years ago. These castles, these palaces, these statues, these pictures that you come here to admire are the work of Italians. Parts of our country may be very poor, but they are very rich in history. Money isn't everything."

If you have understood this point of view, you will have found that the Italians are the kindest and the friendliest of people. They make a lot of noise, they are not good at waiting in queues or at keeping appointments, but they are very ready indeed to help anybody in trouble.

The population of Italy is a little larger than that of England, Scotland and Wales—over fifty-five millions. With its islands, it is considerably bigger than the United Kingdom—116,304 square miles, as against 88,850. But, of course, most of Italy is covered by mountains, where few people can live. Those who do so, tending their sheep or growing their vines, olives and maize, must be among the toughest and most hard-working people in Europe. The land does not produce enough, however hard they work, to keep large families, and some of the younger ones have to emigrate to central Europe, America or Australia in order to make a living. Their family ties are very strong, and many of them send part of their earnings back to the villages in which they

The Pirelli Works, near Naples. Industry is bringing new life to the south

were born and to which they hope to return when they are old.

Northern Italy has become a very important industrial area, with hundreds of new factories in which many of these young men and women from the farms can find work. With the encouragement of the government, many new factories are being built in the poor areas of the south. One result of this, of course, is that fewer Italians in the future will be compelled to go overseas to find work. Their skill will add to the wealth of their own country.

Another result is that the rivalries and misunderstandings between one part of Italy and another, and particularly between the extreme north and the extreme south, are disappearing as the people get to know each other better. It is true that these rivalries were due partly to the geography of Italy—from the very earliest times, foreigners settled in Italy and they kept their ideas, and often their languages, for much longer than they would have done elsewhere because the mountains made it so difficult to meet and to mix with people of other parts of the country.

The mountains also made it difficult for any central government—even the government controlled by the pope in Rome—to enforce order and obedience, so that for centuries the country was split up into small states, often at war with each other. This meant that, although Italy was for so long far ahead of other nations in art and learning, it was behind most of them in government. The fact that it became an independent and united country only about a century ago has hitherto prevented Italy from having as great an influence in world affairs as she should have had. That, too, is changing.

The Italians are lively and demonstrative. They like to talk with their hands as well as with their mouths. They are quick to show their feelings, so that they may suddenly boil up in anger for very little reason. But they are more likely to laugh and sing than to grumble and quarrel. No people in Europe

These primary school town-planners are typical of Italy's future citizens. Like all other Italians, they are quick to smile back

are quicker than they are to answer a smile with a smile.

There is an Italian slang word meaning something like "Hullo!" and also "Cheerio!". The word is *Ciao*! (pronounced "chow"), and it is used a great deal between friends. I hope that, by now, you feel that you know Italy well enough for the Italians to give you that cheerful and friendly greeting.

Index

Abruzzi 71–72
Adriatic Sea 52, 54, 55, 72
Africa, Africans 8, 14, 16, 76
agriculture 46, 48, 50–51, 60, 68–69, 71
Alban Hills 75
Alps 9, 11, 15, 42, 46, 49–50, 63
America, Americans 39, 41, 45, 79–80
Apennines 11, 44, 58, 60, 63, 71
aqueducts 43
area of Italy 90
Arno, R. 40, 66
Asia Minor 8
Austria, Austrians 9, 29, 30, 34
autostrada 43–45, 58, 60, 75

bagpipes 71
banks, banking 28
Bologna 58–60
Britain, British 9, 16, 17, 18, 30, 33, 39
Brunelleschi 66

Caesar, Julius 16, 17, 18, 22
Carrara marble 63
Carthage, Carthaginians 14, 16, 83
Cavour 30–32, 33, 47
Charlemagne, Emperor 25
cheese 50
Christianity 24, 25
Cinque Terre 57
climate 12
Colosseum 20, 23
Constantine, Emperor 24
Corsica 14
Crimean War 32
crops 50, 51, 68–69, 90

Dante 29, 51
da Vinci, Leonardo 66

education 87
Egypt 8
Elba 87–88
England 32, 34
Etruscans 10, 14, 58, 71, 87, 88
explorers 8

Fascism 38, 41
Ferdinand II 33
First World War 38, 39
Florence 16, 28, 35, 40, 60, 66, 70
Fontana di Trevi 74
food 69–70
foreign invaders 7–11, 14, 25, 29, 46, 83
France 9, 15, 39
Franco-Prussian War 36
Frederick II 81
fruit-growing 72

Galileo 51
Games, Roman 14
Garibaldi 30–31, 32, 33–34
Genoa 27–28, 48, 49, 57
Germany 38, 39, 40
Ghibellines 26, 51
Giotto 66
gladiators 20
Greece, Greeks 8, 10, 81, 82
Greek monuments 8, 85
Guelphs 26, 51

94

Hannibal 15–16, 46
Herculaneum 79
hill towns 66–67
Horatio 10

industry 47, 48, 55, 80, 88, 91

Jesus Christ 22–23
Jews 22
Judea 22

Keats, John 73

lakes, Italian 49
language 7, 10, 29, 71, 87

Mafia, the 83, 87
Mazzini 30–31
Medici family 28
Mediterranean Sea 7, 8, 14, 57, 82, 83, 84
Michelangelo 63–65, 66
Milan 12, 44, 47–50
Mont Blanc road tunnel 42, 47
mountains 9, 11, 12, 44, 57, 58, 63, 90, 91
Mussolini 38–39, 41

Naples 29, 32, 33, 44, 47, 76–78
Napoleon Buonaparte 29, 30, 87
Napoleon III 32, 36
natural gas 55
Nazis 38, 39
Normans 83–84

Padua 51
papal states 26, 29, 33, 34, 35, 36
parliament, Italian 41
Petrarch 51
Phoenicians 8, 14
Piedmont 30, 31, 47
Pisa, leaning tower of 65
Po, R. 47, 50, 52, 54, 55
Pompeii 79
Pompey 17

Ponte Vecchio 40
pope, popes 25–26, 30, 35, 36, 37, 91
population:
  Italy 7, 90
  Milan 47
  Naples 47
  Rome 25
  Turin 47
Portofino 57
poverty 70, 77–78, 80–81, 83

Redshirts 33
Reggio Calabria 44, 58
Remus 10
Renaissance (*Rinascimento*) 66, 72, 73
Riomaggiori 57
Riviera, Italian 49, 54, 57
Rome, Romans 10, 13, 14, 15, 16, 17, 18,
  22, 24, 25, 35, 36, 38, 43, 48, 57, 60,
  66, 71, 72–74
Roman Baths 18–19
Roman Empire 16, 17, 18, 24
Romulus 10

San Marino, Republic of 67–68
Sardinia 14, 84, 85
Second World War 39–40, 55
Senate 17
sheep 61, 71, 90
Sicily 8, 14, 32, 33, 39, 81, 82–85, 86
Sienna 70–71
silk 16–17, 50
Simplon railway tunnel 42
Spain, Spaniards 15, 29, 84
Spanish steps 73
sports 12
St Bernard road tunnel 42, 47
St Peter's church 37, 65, 72
Switzerland 9

Tiber, R. 10, 13, 66, 74
trade 10, 16
Trasimene, Lake 15
trees 50, 60, 69
Trieste 49

Turin 47–48, 50, 55
Tuscany 10, 60

unity of Italy 30, 32, 33, 35–36, 37, 41, 92

Vatican 37, 72, 73
Venice 27, 28, 34, 48, 49, 50, 51–57
Vesuvius, M. 78–79
Via Aurelia 46

Victor Emmanuel II 31, 32, 33, 34, 35–36, 47
Victor Emmanuel III 38
Victoria, Queen 34
vines, vineyards 50, 57, 60, 68

wild animals 71–72
wine 68–69